Wea

MW01602215

Written by Margie Burton, Catl

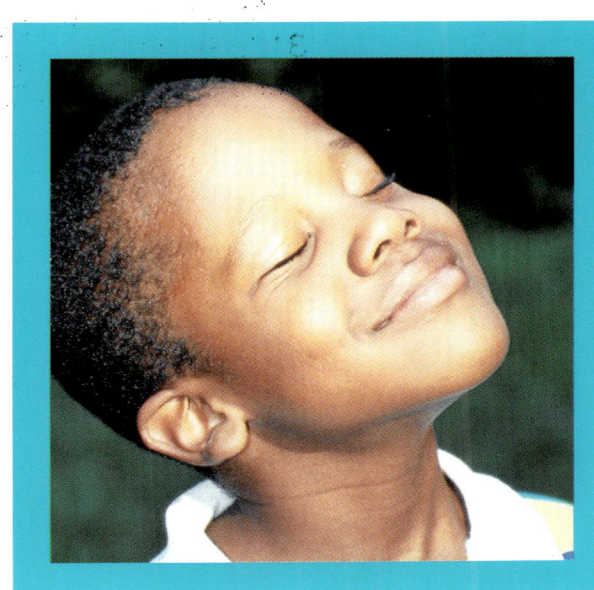

Look at the thermometer.

I can read the temperature.

We look at the thermometer when we go out.

3

Today is a hot day. There are no clouds in the sky.

Look at the clouds. They
are made of drops
of water. These water drops
are too little to see.
This is where the rain begins.

This is lightning. It is
a big flash of light.

It begins at
the clouds and
goes down to
the ground.

Today is windy. See how the wind blows the clothes?

See the tornado? The wind is going around very fast. This is a very big storm.

Today is very cold. Look at the frost on the flower. It is made when the water on the ground gets cold.

Look at the snow!

15

It is raining today. We
go out in our raincoats.